Kids of the BIBLE Storybook

12 Biblical Children Whose Stories
Demonstrate God's Love

written by Franklin Goldberg   illustrated by Kaitlyn Goldberg

Joseph was very special in God's eyes

When he was a teen, he had a SPECTACULAR dream
   of stars, the sun, and the moon.
That dream foretold
   that before he was old,
he'd become a great man
   destined to rescue the land
and deliver God's people from harm.

Over the years,
   he helped calm many fears
By explaining more dreams
   which were not what they seemed.

Joseph's special gift from above
   was a sign of God's unfailing love;
Just like every talent he gives people today
   makes each of us useful in our own special way.

Moses was very special in God's eyes

When he was a baby,
    things were dangerous and scary.
So, the mother of this child
    left her son in the Nile;
Trusting God would do
    something miraculous, something new.

The basket in which he was laid
    was discovered by a royal maid.
She brought him to a princess
    who raised him as her own
And just as Moses's mother had hoped,
    God's faithfulness was shown.

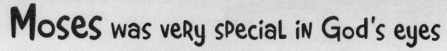

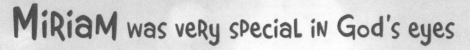

MIRIAM was very special in God's eyes

When she was a young girl,
   she watched her mother trust God with her brother
Patiently, she waited at the riverside,
   eager to see how God would provide.
When the princess found Moses, she bravely came near
   and offered a suggestion, a clever idea.

"Would you like some help to raise the babe
   just till he's a bit older, a more manageable age?"

When the princess agreed, Miriam sprang to her feet
   chose her mom for the job – now God's miracle was complete!

Samuel was very special in God's eyes

Even before his birth
   God showed Samuel his worth.
When his mother prayed for a son
   she asked for just one,
And promised to give him right back
   to serve God – that was her pact.

God heard her appeal
   and agreed to the deal.
To the temple, Samuel was brought
   where he did what he was taught.

One night, the Lord called him by name
   and invited him to proclaim
His words and his truth
   even during his youth.

From beginning to end,
   Samuel's life was on lend
To a God who deserved
   to be faithfully served.

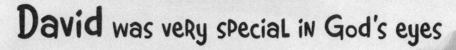

David was very special in God's eyes

When he was a lad,
    he watched sheep for his dad.
Each night he took such care,
    even fought off a lion and a bear.
As a teen, he faced a giant with just a sling and a stone
    God honored his bravery and gave him the throne

David found many ways
    to serve God and give him praise.
As a shepherd, soldier, king, songwriter, and musician,
    pleasing God in all he did became his sole mission.

His deep love for the Lord set him apart
    and earned him the title – A man after God's own heart.

A young friend of Elijah
was very special in God's eyes

When Elijah first met a widow and her son,
   they were about to eat a meal – their last one.
There were all out of food,
   and although it seemed rude
Elijah asked for the last bite,
   but he promised that night
That if they gave up this meal
   they'd get quite a deal.

The claim that he made
   was more than a fair trade.
Exchange one meal for many,
   he vowed they'd have plenty.

They believed and were blessed
   for having listened to their guest
Every day food suddenly appeared
   and it lasted for 2 years,
All because the widow and her lad
   gave up all they had.

A young girl in Elisha's Day

was very special in God's eyes

When she was a young maid
 she was scared and afraid.
Far from home and her land
 but with God she did stand.

When Naaman became ill
 she was filled with good will
And told him of a prophet renowned
 and where he could be found.

Elisha's methods seemed strange
 but Naaman's body was changed.
After washing himself seven times in a row,
 he stepped out of the river with skin all aglow

Naaman's healing was due
 to Elisha's miracle, that is true.
But he only found himself cured
 because this girl's voice was heard.

Daniel was very special in God's eyes

When he was just a boy,
    he had to make a hard choice.
Daniel and three of his friends
    were offered food that offends
So, they took a bold stand
    against the ruler of the land.

All four boys resolved to not eat
    even one bite of the king's meat.
Instead they ate only veggies and water
    and trusted God to help their bodies grow stronger.

After ten days had passed
    God gave them what they asked.
They were healthy and fit,
    strong in body and in wit.
No one else could compare,
    because God answered their prayer.

Shadrach, Meshach, and Abednego
were very special in God's eyes

When Daniel's three friends were tested again
  they remained faithful and true
Refusing to worship the king's golden statue.

Their punishment was severe
  and as the soldiers came near
All hope was lost
  when into a fiery furnace they were tossed.

But much to everyone's surprise
  Jesus appeared before their eyes.
He kept them safe and unharmed
  secure in his arms.

Not one hair on their heads
  nor their clothes' smallest threads
Were singed in the flame
  because they honored God's name.

The son of a Nobleman
was very special in Jesus' eyes

When he was terribly sick
   his father acted real quick.
As soon as he learned that Jesus was near
   he ran to meet him, eyes filled with tears.

After hearing the father's appeal
   for his son to be healed,
Jesus did something rare
   and healed him right there.
Without visiting his town or sitting by his bed,
   Jesus healed the distant boy just as he said.

Children were very special in Jesus' eyes

One day a huge crowd gathered 'round
    to hear his words, so profound.
But no one thought ahead,
    to bring lunch, even bread.

Then a boy offered to share
    the small meal he had prepared.
Two fishes and five loaves
    miraculously fed the people in droves,
Leaving baskets of leftovers behind
    all because this boy was so kind.

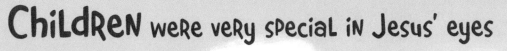

CHILDREN WERE VERY SPECIAL IN Jesus' eyes and Jesus WAS VERY SPECIAL to them

When he rode into Jerusalem on a donkey one day
they gathered to see him and hear what he might say.
The kids were filled with such joy and delight,
they waved palm branches and sang with all their might.

Their little voices of praise gave Jesus such pleasure,
because to him and his father, every child is a treasure!

Like all these children from God's Word,
   every little one today can rest assured
That God knows you by name
   and he loves you the same.
What a wonderful surprise
   to know **you** are very special in God's eyes!

About the Author and Illustrator

The author and illustrator of *The Kids of the Bible Storybook* are a father/daughter team. Kaitlyn (the illustrator) was born prematurely, weighing only 3 pounds, 4 ounces. Each day, her father, Franklin (the author) visited her in the hospital, where he held her tiny hand while quietly singing *Jesus Loves Me* as a prayer for God to keep Kaitlyn strong and healthy.

Little ones to him belong. They are weak, but he is strong.

God answered those prayers and kept her safe. This book rose out of Franklin and Kaitlyn's personal story of experiencing the reality of how special children are in God's eyes.

Their hope is that these 12 stories of kids in the Bible will encourage children to experience God's love for themselves and that they will carry that confidence with them throughout their lives.

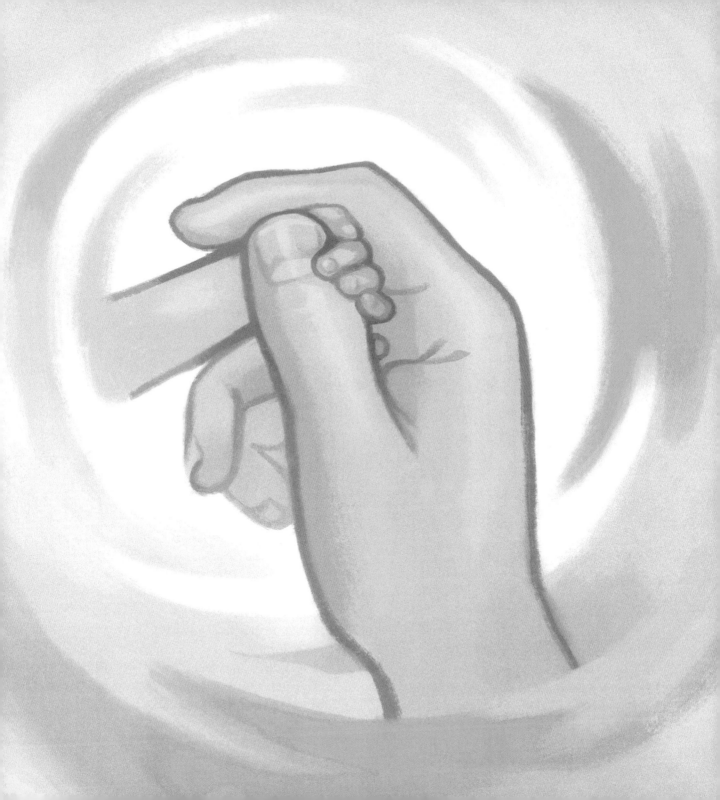

Parent Guide

Tips for Using the Parent Guide

The Parent Guide includes Scripture References, Family Discussion ideas, and Prayer Prompts for each of the 12 stories contained within the *Kids of the Bible Storybook*. A downloadable & printable edition is also available at KidsoftheBible.com.

To get the most from the Parent Guide, we recommend the following:

- Read one or more of the Scripture passages with your children that contain the stories from the book

- Go through those passages yourself first before reading them with your child. Consider the age and unique sensitivities of children when deciding which verses should be read, explained, or skipped.

- Review the options listed in the Family Discussion section and choose one or two of the topics that are most relevant to you and your child. There are enough options to go back through and repeat the process multiple times.

- Review the prayer prompts and choose one to guide you and your child's prayers.

- Download free coloring pages at KidsoftheBible.com to offer more ways for your child to engage with these stories.

Scripture Index

Scripture References for the Stories within *The Kids of the Bible Storybook*:

1. Joseph: Genesis 37:1-11
2. Moses: Exodus 2:1-10
3. Miriam: Exodus 2:1-10
4. Samuel: 1 Samuel 3:1-21
5. David: 1 Samuel 17:12-50
6. The Son of the Widow of Zarephath: 1 Kings 17:8-16
7. The Maid of Naaman: 2 Kings 5:1-14
8. Daniel: Daniel 1:1-21
9. Shadrach, Meshach, and Abednego: Daniel 3:1-30
10. The Son of a Nobleman: John 4:43-54
11. The Boy with Loaves & Fishes: John 6:1-13
12. Children at Jesus' Triumphal Entry: Matthew 21:1-16

10 Scripture References Regarding God's Special Love for Children:

1. God heard the cries of baby Ishmael: Genesis 21:17
2. Children are a gift from God: Psalm 127:3
3. God forms children in the womb: Psalm 139:13-16
4. Jesus used a child as an example of faith: Matthew 18:2-6
5. Jesus said children have guardian angels: Matthew 18:10
6. Jesus said that his Father cares for every single child: Matthew 18:12-14
7. Jesus prayed for children: Matthew 19:13-15
8. Jesus said that generosity towards children is the same as generosity towards him: Mark 9:36-37
9. Jesus held children in his arms: Mark 10:13-16
10. Pure religion includes helping children in need: James 1:27

The Story of Joseph

Scripture References:

- Joseph's dreams: Genesis 37:1-11
- Joseph's time as a servant: Genesis 39:1-18
- Joseph's years in prison: Genesis 39:19-23
- Joseph's dream fulfilled: Genesis 41:37-46

Family Discussion:

God has a plan for each of our lives:
- Read Jeremiah 29:11
- God had a plan for Joseph's life even when he was a child. How does it make you feel to know God has a plan for your life too? How should this impact our choices in life?

God's plan often includes difficulties:
- God's plan for Joseph's life included many challenges and setbacks
- How do you think Joseph felt when those divine dreams didn't come true year after year? Do you think he had seasons where disappointment, frustration or anger overwhelmed him?
- How might God have used these challenges to develop Joseph's character so he could be the leader God intended him to be?

God is present with us during tough times:
- In Genesis 39:2, the Bible says that God was with Joseph when he was a servant to Potiphar and that God helped Joseph succeed in everything he did.
- In Genesis 39:21, the Bible says that God was with Joseph in the prison, showing him faithful love.
- Although Joseph suffered unfair treatment, God never left him and never stopped caring for him. He was faithful and gave Joseph strength and opportunities to succeed even during difficult times.
- How can we remember to rely on God's presence and love when things aren't going well?

We can focus on helping others even when we're hurting ourselves:
- Who do you know who is sad and could use encouragement?
- How could you help them feel better?

Prayer Prompts:

- Thank God that he has a plan for your child's life
- Ask God for help to be patient and to trust him when we feel alone
- Pray for someone who is sad and needs encouragement
- Pray for God's plan for your children to be made clear as they grow up

The Story of Moses

Scripture References:

- Moses' birth and God's protection: Exodus 2:1-10
- Moses' calling at the burning bush: Exodus 3:1-22, Exodus 4:1-17
- Moses' return to Egypt: Exodus 4:18-31
- Moses' plea for Israel's freedom: Exodus 5:1-23
- Moses and the Exodus: Exodus 12:31-42
- Moses parts the Red Sea: Exodus 14:1-31

Family Discussion:

God cares for and protects children:
- God miraculously cared for Moses as a baby in that basket and he still miraculously protects children today.
- Matthew 18:10 says that children have guardian angels protecting them.
- In what ways does God protect children? Think of big and small ways that he works through others and behind the scenes to protect kids.

Consider Moses' humble beginnings:
- Moses was helpless as an infant in that basket placed in the river. He was completely dependent on God to protect him, and that humble dependence became a dominant trait of Moses' life.
- Numbers 12:3 says Moses was very humble. In fact, it says that he was the most humble person on the planet!
- In what ways are we completely dependent on God? (Acts 17:28, Acts 17:24-25, Isaiah 42:5)

Discuss the reliance Moses' mother had on God to protect her son:
- When she placed Moses in the basket and laid it in the river, she was completely trusting God to do something she could no longer do – protect her son.
- Think of one specific thing we can't do ourselves that we need to trust God to do for us.

Prayer Prompts:

- Thank God for protecting us every day in big and small ways
- Ask God for the grace to be humble and to remember how dependent we are on him
- Pray for that one specific thing we need to trust God to do for us

The Story of Miriam

Scripture References:
- Miriam's childhood bravery: Exodus 2:1-10
- Miriam's leadership in worship and song: Exodus 15:20-21

Family Discussion:

Discuss Miriam's important role in Moses' story:
- When Miriam watched her mother place her baby brother in the river, she was compelled to stay and see what would happen next.
- Had she not stayed and intervened, Moses' story wouldn't have been the same.
- As a child, Miriam played an important role in God's plan. Children don't need to wait to grow up before they can do important things for God!

Consider how those who start serving God as children can grow to serve him their whole lives:
- Miriam continued to serve God in a variety of important ways throughout her life.
- She became a worship leader who played the tambourine and led a group of women who praised God together after they were delivered from Egypt (Exodus 15:20).
- In Exodus 15:20, she is called "Miriam the prophet," so she had another important role of bringing God's messages to his people.

Discuss ways that, like Miriam, we are also called to help others:
- Micah 6:4 says that God sent Miriam and her siblings as a gift to help God's people.
- Think of one specific way God could use you to help someone today.

Discuss the joy of serving God together as a family:
- When Miriam, her brother Moses, and her other brother, Aaron, grew up, they all served God together.
- In what ways can you serve God this week with siblings, parents, or other relatives?

Prayer Prompts:
- Thank God for using us in ways that make a difference in the lives of other people. Thank God for the family he has given you to serve him with.
- Ask God to help your child see opportunities to serve God this week
- Pray for blessing upon the areas in which you choose to serve God together as a family

The Story of Samuel

Scripture References:
- Samuel's miraculous birth: 1 Samuel 1:1-23
- Samuel's childhood service at the temple: 1 Samuel 1:24-28, 1 Samuel 2:18-22, 26
- Samuel hears the voice of God: 1 Samuel 3:1-21

Family Discussion Topics:

Children don't need to wait to grow up before they can serve God:
- 1 Samuel 2:18 says that, even though he was only a boy, Samuel served God.
- What ways can you serve God this week?

Discuss the importance of choosing to serve God:
- Samuel's mother dedicated him to the Lord before he was born, but Samuel still had to choose for himself if he was going to believe.
- When he heard God's voice, he chose to believe and serve the God of his mother.
- Discuss how each child needs to make their own decision to believe and trust God.

Consider Samuel's full life of service to God:
- Samuel grew up to serve God in many different ways. He became a prophet, a judge, and a priest for the nation of Israel. Samuel even anointed David as king!
- Samuel's commitment to serve God as a child gave him a lifetime of exciting opportunities to do things that matter.
- Ask your child what ways they would want to serve God as they get older.

Prayer Prompts:
- Thank God for the positive example of parents and family members who believe in Jesus
- Ask God to help your children make their own choice to believe in God
- Pray for God to give each child a life full of exciting opportunities to serve him

The Story of David

Scripture References:

- David's service as a shepherd: 1 Samuel 17:34-37
- David's anointing to become the king: 1 Samuel 16:1-13
- David's service to the king through music: 1 Samuel 16:14-23
- David and Goliath: 1 Samuel 17:1-50
- David becomes king: 2 Samuel 5:1-5

Family Discussion:

Discuss David's faithfulness:

- As a child, David showed faithfulness in his job as a shepherd boy, guarding his father's sheep. That faithfulness grew as God trusted him with a bigger role of being a shepherd and protector for his people - the entire nation of Israel.
- David served God in many ways throughout his life – as a musician, songwriter, soldier, father, and king.
- Discuss how a child's faithfulness can grow and lead to more opportunities to serve him throughout their lives.

Consider David's heart for God:

- In 1 Samuel 13:14 and Acts 13:22, David is referred to as a man after God's own heart. David cared about the things that God cared about. He was passionate for God, his Word, and his people.
- How can we be people after God's own heart today?

Consider David's bravery:

- David was able to bravely face Goliath because he had already experienced God's protection when his flock of sheep was attacked by a lion and a bear.
- Seeing God provide in small things can help us trust him with bigger things later.
- Discuss a few specific small blessings God has given to you and your family recently and discuss how that should help you trust him for the bigger things.

Prayer Prompts:

- Thank God for the specific examples of small blessings God has given to us
- Ask God to help you trust him when you face larger needs
- Pray for your child to be a person after God's own heart

The Story of the Son of the Widow of Zarephath

Scripture References:

- The widow and her son's generosity: 1 Kings 17:8-16
- The widow's son is raised from the dead: 1 Kings 17:17-24

Family Discussion:

Discuss the widow and her son's sacrifice:

- Consider another widow's generous example from the New Testament (Luke 21:1-4). She gave a small amount of money, but, like the widow of Zarephath, it was all that she had left.
- The widow and her son only had enough food for one more meal. How do you think they felt when Elisha asked for it?
- Sometimes a decision to be generous or obedient to God impacts the entire family. This was more than just the widow's act of faith, it was also her son's. How might we as a family decide to demonstrate generosity and faith together?

Consider the reward for their sacrifice:

- The widow and her son received hundreds and hundreds of meals in exchange for the one they gave to Elijah. God is capable of blessing us in ways that are far greater than anything he asks us to give up (see Ephesians 3:20,21).
- Discuss what the widow and her son's daily experience must have been like as they reached into the barrel and pulled out food that wasn't there the night before. Do you think they laughed? Do you think they tried to catch it happening? Do you think there was a special sound or glow when it was replenished?

Talk about daily bread:

- Although the widow and her son received hundreds of meals, they didn't get it all at once. God didn't fill a barn with food. They received just enough for each day.
- Consider the similar story of how God provided manna for the Israelites each morning, but it was just enough for that day's needs (Exodus 16:4).
- Read the Lord's Prayer (Matthew 6:9-13) and discuss how Jesus instructs us to ask for food for each day.
- In what other ways (besides food) does God want us to depend on him daily?

Prayer Prompts:

- Thank God for providing for today's needs
- Ask God to help you trust him with your future needs
- Pray for opportunities to help others in need

The Story of the Young Maid

Scripture Reference:
- 2 Kings 5:1-14

Family Discussion:
Discuss the importance of caring for others:
- This young girl had to deal with sudden change when she moved from her hometown to live with Naaman and his family. But even amidst that chaos, she cared about the needs of those around her and did her best to help.
- When we are having a bad day, what can we do to make sure we pay attention to the needs of others?

Discuss this young girl's courage and bravery:
- It took courage for this young girl to speak up and recommend the prophet Elisha. She was in an unfamiliar place and wasn't with her friends and family. It would have been easy to be shy and silent. But she cared enough to speak up and offer to help.
- What are some examples of times when we're tempted to be shy and quiet? How can we prepare ourselves to speak up when it can help others?

Discuss this young girl's strong faith:
- This young girl had tremendous faith. She heard stories of how God was using Elisha to do exciting things, and her faith in God's power to heal motivated her to take the risk of recommending that Naaman go see him.

Discuss how God uses the faith of children to accomplish great things.
- This young girl's belief saved Naaman's life! We don't have to wait to become teenagers or adults to do great things for God that make a difference in the world! This remarkable story made its way into the Bible because children are special in God's eyes, and they can make a difference at any age.

Prayer Prompts:
- Thank God for each child in your family and how they have been a blessing to you and others
- Ask God for help to discover ways to bless others even when we're having a bad day
- Pray for those you know who are not feeling well and ask for God's healing

The Story of Daniel

Scripture References:
- Daniel and his friends stand for God in their youth: Daniel 1:1-21
- Daniel interprets the king's dreams: Daniel 2:1-49, Daniel 4:1-37
- Daniel and the writing on the wall: Daniel 5:1-29
- Daniel and the lions' den: Daniel 6:1-28

Family Discussion:
Discuss the benefits of having good friends:
- Read Ecclesiastes 4:9-12
- Daniel and his 3 friends were in a scary situation, but together they found the courage to stand for what was right.
- Ask your child to share a story of a time a friend encouraged them recently.
- Ask your child to think of a friend who needs help or encouragement and make a list of ways they can help.

Discuss specific ways to serve God with friends:
- Make a short list of specific things your child can do with their friends this week that would be a blessing to someone else.

Prayer Prompts:
- Thank God for specific friends of your children
- Ask God to use your child and their friends to be a blessing to each other and to others around them
- Pray for the needs of 2-3 of your children's closest friends

The Story of Shadrach, Meshach, and Abednego

Scripture References:
- Daniel, Shadrach, Meshach, and Abednego stand together: Daniel 1:1-21
- The fiery furnace: Daniel 3:1-30

Family Discussion:
Discuss the danger of peer pressure:
- These 3 friends were under tremendous pressure to comply with what the rest of the country was doing. They were the only ones who chose to obey God.
- Discuss the power of peer pressure to go with the flow, even when you don't feel right about it.

Discuss what it must have been like for these friends to see Jesus:
- Appearances of Jesus before his birth were very rare!
- Discuss how special it was for Jesus to come down and be with these 3 friends during this time.

Discuss the blessings of having Jesus with us on our bad days:
- Even though we can't see Jesus, he is just as much with us during our bad days as he was with these 3 friends.
- Read these verses about God's presence with us: Psalm 46:1, Psalm 41:10, Isaiah 41:10,13, Deuteronomy 31:6

Prayer Prompts:
- Thank God for always being with us
- Ask God for courage to obey him even when no one else around us is being obedient
- Pray for people you know who are going through tough times and need to feel and rest in God's presence

The Story of the Nobleman's Son

Scripture Reference:
- John 4:43-54

Family Discussion:
Discuss the importance of letting God answer prayer his way:
- The nobleman had a plan for how he wanted Jesus to heal his son. He expected that it would require a personal visit from Jesus to his home. He was shocked when Jesus offered a different way to answer his prayer, but he believed and returned home to see his prayers answered.
- Discuss how God's plans for answering our prayers are often not the same as our plans. Share some stories of how this has happened in your life, especially when God's plan was so much better than your original one.

Discuss the lasting impact this miracle may have had on the boy's life:
- How do you think this boy's life was affected by this miraculous healing? Do you think he became famous in his town? Do you think he lived differently because his life was saved by God?

Discuss how God still answers prayer without being physically present in a given situation:
- God still answers prayers today, doing miraculous things all over the world because of the prayers of his people (James 5:16). Just as Jesus didn't need to be physically present to heal the boy, he doesn't need to be present to answer prayers all over the world today.

Make a short list of things to pray for related to people who aren't geographically close to you (family, friends, entire countries experiencing difficulties).

Prayer Prompts:
- Thank God and praise him for being everywhere all the time so that he can help people all over the world
- Ask God for faith to trust him to answer our prayers in his own way
- Pray for the specific needs of people who are not physically near you (i.e., distant relatives, missionaries serving in another country)

The Story of the Boy Who Shared His Lunch

Scripture Reference:
- John 6:1-13

Family Discussion:

Discuss how the boy might have felt:
- How do you think this boy felt when Andrew saw him, noticed his lunch, approached him, and asked if he would consider giving his lunch to Jesus?
- Do you think he was nervous? Shy? Confused? Reluctant to share his food? Worried that his parents might be upset that he gave away his lunch?
- How do you think he felt when Andrew brought him right up to meet Jesus in person?

Discuss God's ability to multiply our gifts today:
- The food that this boy shared was multiplied many thousands of times over.
- How can God take something small that we give him today and use it in bigger ways than we can imagine?

Discuss the impact this miracle may have had on this boy's life:
- How do you think this miracle affected the boy's life? Did he look for more ways to be generous?

Make a list of 2-3 small things that you can do this week to meet someone else's need. Focus on small needs (a meal, a card, a visit, a note, a phone call, a small gift) and then pray for God to bless what you give.

Prayer Prompts:
- Thank God that he uses us in ways that are greater than ourselves
- Ask God for opportunities to share generously with others
- Pray for God to bless the specific small things that you decided to do for others

The Story of Children Singing at Jesus' Triumphal Entry

Scripture Reference:
- Matthew 21:1-16

Family Discussion:

Discuss the prophecy of this event:
- Read Psalm 8 and emphasize the prophecy found in verse 2.
- It was God's plan for Jesus's life on earth to begin and end with a chorus of singing. At his birth, he was welcomed by a chorus of angels (Luke 2:8-15) and near the end of his life, a chorus of children welcomed him into Jerusalem.
- What a special thing that God's plan for this moment in history involved the songs of children!

Discuss how God loves to hear children sing to him:
- Talk about how our songs are not only heard by those around us, but they are heard and loved by Jesus.
- Consider discussing how a lack of vocal talent doesn't impact God's joy in hearing us praise him.

If not already a part of your family devotion time, consider singing to God each day as a family.

Choose a song or two to sing together before you pray.

Prayer Prompts:
- Thank God for being tender and compassionate - for taking pleasure in our songs of praise
- Ask God to help you remember he is listening each time you sing to him
- Pray for your next church service - that the entire congregation's worship would bring God great joy